SIAMESE CATS

by Mari Schuh

AMICUS HIGH INTEREST • AMICUS INK

Amicus High Interest and Amicus Ink are imprints of Amicus
P.O. Box 1329, Mankato, MN 56002
www.amicuspublishing.us

Library of Congress Cataloging-in-Publication Data
Schuh, Mari C., 1975- author.
Siamese cats / by Mari Schuh.
    pages cm. -- (Favorite cat breeds)
Audience: K to grade 3.
Summary: "A photo-illustrated book for early readers about Siamese cats. Describes the Siamese's unique features, history as good show cats, social behaviors, and how they act as pets"-- Provided by publisher.
Includes bibliographical references and index.
ISBN 978-1-60753-972-8 (library binding)
ISBN 978-1-68152-101-5 (pbk.)
ISBN 978-1-68151-006-4 (ebook)
1. Siamese cat--Juvenile literature. 2. Cat breeds--Juvenile literature. I. Title.
SF449.S5S38 2017
636.8'25--dc23
                    2015028810

Photo Credits: Erik Lam / Shutterstock cover; GlobalP / iStock 2, 8-9; Jean Michel Labat / ardea.com / Pantheon / Superstock 5; Nuttapong Wongcheronkit / Alamy 6; Eivaisla / iStock 10-11; Christina Gandolfo / Alamy 13; catman73 / iStock 14-15; Gaertner / Alamy 17; parkerphotography / Alamy 18; studio22comua / iStock 20-21; Julia Remezova / Shutterstock 22

Editor: Wendy Dieker
Designer: Tracy Myers
Photo Researcher: Rebecca Bernin

Printed in the United States of America.

HC 10 9 8 7 6 5 4 3 2 1
PB 10 9 8 7 6 5 4 3 2 1

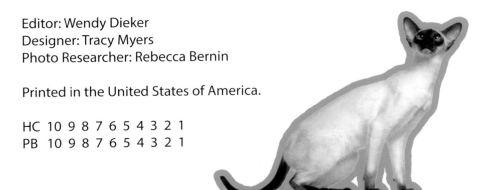

TABLE OF CONTENTS

BEAUTIFUL CATS

A beautiful cat purrs. It closely follows its owner. Then it climbs and jumps. The cat is long and thin. It is a Siamese.

Fun Fact
Siamese cats are called "Meezers." The nickname comes from the last part of their name.

50 สต.
ST
POSTAGE
ประเทศไทย THAILAN
SIAMESE CAT
CHOCOLATE POINT
แต้มสีน้ำตาล

HISTORY

Siamese cats were popular long ago. They lived in a country called Siam. Siam is now called Thailand. These cats may have lived with monks and royalty.

LONG AND THIN

Siamese cats are long. Their bodies are lean, but strong. They have thin legs and long necks. These cats also have long, thin tails.

BLUE-EYED CATS

Siamese cats have **slanted** blue eyes. Their noses are long and straight. They have big, pointed ears. Their heads are shaped like a triangle.

SHORT FUR

Siamese cats have short, shiny fur.
It is silky. A Siamese's **coat** is a light
color. The cat has darker fur on its
face, ears, legs, and tail.

13

KITTENS

Mother Siamese cats have big **litters**. They often have three to six kittens at a time. The kittens are born with white fur. Later, some of their fur darkens.

Like a Wild Cat?
Mother housecats feed their kittens milk, just like mother wild cats do.

GROOMING

Siamese are easy to **groom**. They need to be combed once a week. They can also be groomed with wet hands. This gets rid of loose hairs.

CURIOUS CATS

Siamese cats can be **moody**. Some days they do not want to play. But other days, they act like dogs. They play fetch. They also learn tricks. These cats are smart and **curious**.

Like a Wild Cat?
Housecats can be active at night, like wild cats. But housecats can learn to rest at night.

LOUD BUT LOVING

Siamese cats meow a lot. They also howl. They can sound like a crying baby. Siamese are loud and noisy. But they are loving, **loyal** pets.

HOW DO YOU KNOW IT'S A SIAMESE?

triangle-shaped head

slanted blue eyes

long, straight nose

light fur on body

long, thin tail

dark fur on legs, tail, and face

WORDS TO KNOW

coat – an animal's hair or fur

curious – eager to learn and find out about new things

groom – to take care of and to clean

litter – a group of animals born at the same time to one mother

loyal – being true and faithful to someone

moody – unhappy or gloomy

slanted – sloped or at an angle

LEARN MORE

Books

Felix, Rebecca. *Siamese*. Cool Cats. Minneapolis: Bellwether Media, 2016.

Meister, Cari. *Cats*. My First Pet. Minneapolis: Bullfrog Books, 2015.

Websites

Cat Fanciers' Association: For Kids
kids.cfa.org/index.html

CATS Protection: All About Cats
www.cats.org.uk//cats-for-kids/about-cats/

INDEX